SAY, SPELL A
WRITE

by

E. W. ELLIS

STANLEY THORNES
(PUBLISHERS) LTD

First edition published in 1982 by

Stanley Thornes (Publishers) Ltd
Educa House
Old Station Drive
off Leckhampton Road
CHELTENHAM GL53 ODN

British Library Cataloguing in Publication Data

Ellis, E.W.
Say, spell and write.
1. English grammar
I. Title
428 PE1112

ISBN 0-85950-373-9

Typeset in 12/16 pt Univers Medium Educational
by Quadraset Limited, Radstock, Bath, Avon BA3 3AN

Printed in Great Britain by Ebenezer Baylis & Son Ltd, Worcester and London

1

sh and **ch**

ship

chur**ch**

1.	Part of a tree.	bran**
2.	A place where goods are sold.	**op
3.	More than one child.	**ildren
4.	The opposite of poor.	ri**
5.	Like a small tree.	bu**
6.	An American cattle farm.	ran**
7.	They swim in seas and lakes.	fi**
8.	Sailors work on board them.	**ips
9.	A kind of nut.	**estnut
10.	A game played by two people.	**ess
11.	Collections of flowers.	bun**es
12.	A boxer may be punched on it.	**in
13.	A kind of bird.	fin**
14.	It helps to make things shine.	poli**
15.	The outside part of a nut.	**ell

16. Stan and Tom are **ums. They often **at to ea** other about the holiday whi** they had together last year. They stayed at a hotel near a sandy bea**. Stan's father had taken them fi**ing in a small fi**ing boat. The fi** whi** they caught was sold at the fi** market. The owner of the local fi** and **ip **op bought all their fi**. When they bought some fi** and **ips at that **op on the following day they wondered if they were eating the fi** whi** Stan's father had caught.

2

sh and **th**

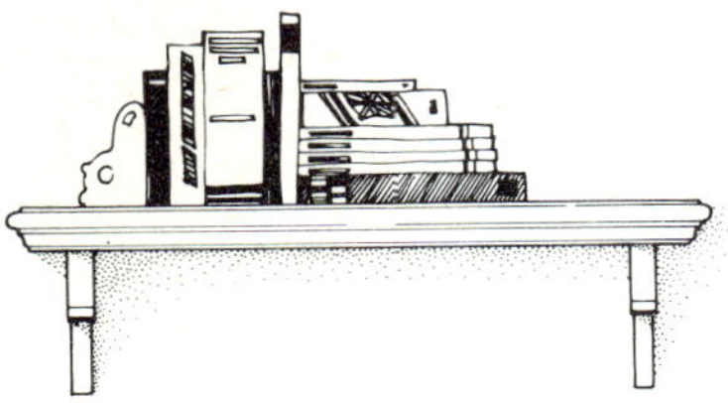

shelf

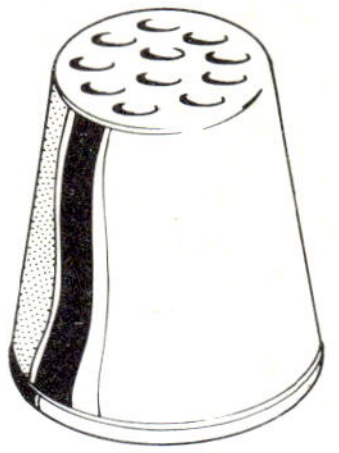

thimble

1. Anglers are people who try to catch fi**.
2. A mo** looks like a kind of butterfly.
3. Peter keeps his pocket money in a ca** box.
4. Some rose bu**es have long **orns.
5. Very big **ips often have two funnels.
6. You should bru** your tee** after every meal.
7. Teacher keeps her books on a wooden **elf.
8. A **rush is singing high up in that tree.
9. Greengrocers sell fre** fruit and vegetables.
10. Fa**er dug the garden yesterday morning.
11. Mother put some clean towels in the ba**room.
12. Ruth threw three coins into the wi**ing well.
13. Did you hear the sound of **under last night?
14. Plants wi**er and die if they have no water.
15. The **in man is wearing a brown clo** cap.

shower

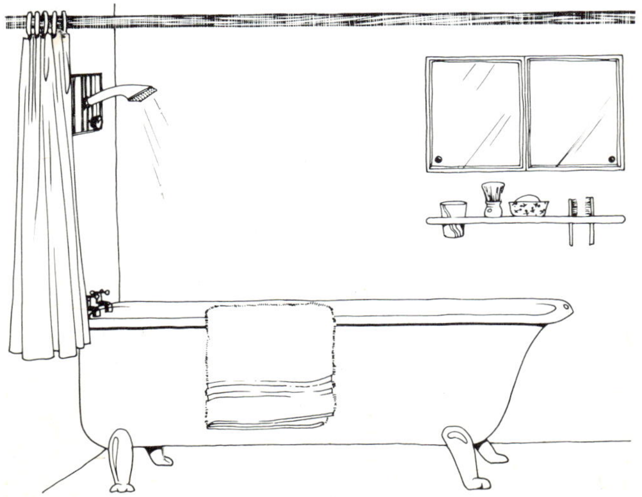

bathroom cabinet

toothbrush
shaving brush

bath

3

ch and **ck**

children

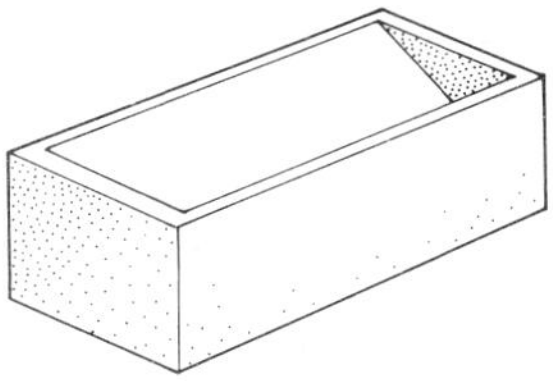

bri**ck**

1.	A long wooden seat.	ben**
2.	Footsteps left by animals.	tra**s
3.	A collection of grapes.	bun**
4.	Young people.	**ildren
5.	A kind of large bag.	sa**
6.	Part of a tree.	bran**
7.	These eggs are sold cheaply.	cra**ed
8.	A kind of coat.	ja**et
9.	Quick light meals.	sna**s
10.	Part of a belt.	bu**le
11.	This bird is seen in some clocks.	cu**oo
12.	Another kind of bird.	chaffin**
13.	An African ape.	**impanzee
14.	Bells do this.	**ime
15.	A wild dog.	ja**al

ducks
necks
pecking

children
chickens

4

ing and ong

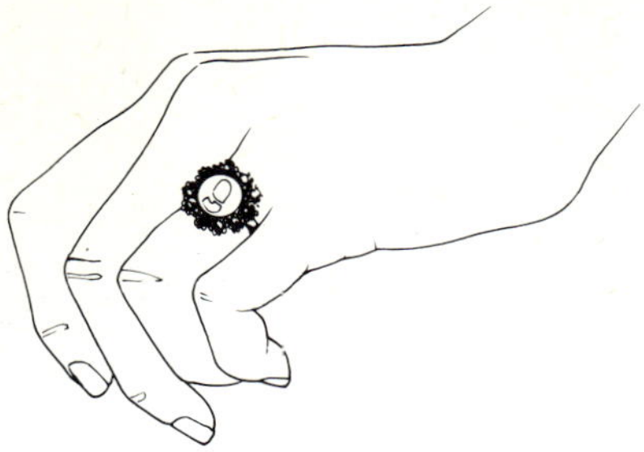

ring

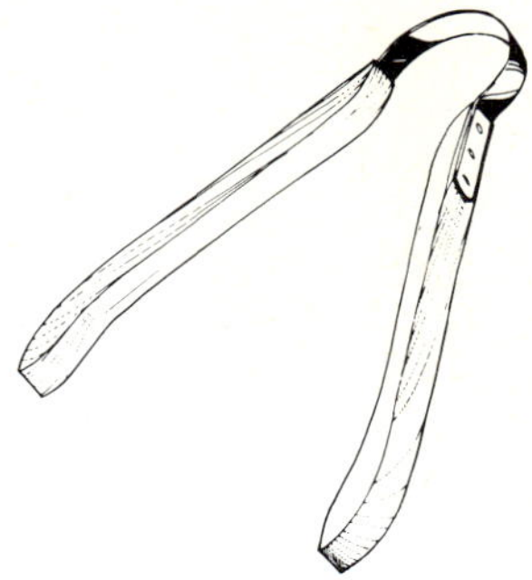

tongs

1. Jenny has a gold r*** on her f***er.
2. The cat is playing with a ball of str***.
3. It is a l*** distance from Spain to Japan.
4. Most children like to s*** happy s***s.
5. Some goats are standing am*** the sheep.
6. A sw*** hangs from a branch of that tree.
7. Please br*** me some potatoes from the garden.
8. A cat cl***s to a tree with its claws.
9. Lions and tigers bel*** to the cat family.
10. Angry bees and wasps may st*** you.
11. Careless children sometimes write wr*** answers.
12. Str*** men can lift heavy weights.
13. S***le people are persons who have not married.
14. A starl*** with a broken w*** cannot fly.
15. T***s may be used for lifting lumps of sugar.

16. There is a l*** path lead*** to the bottom of Anne's garden. A str*** oak tree grows near the end of the path. A sw*** hangs from the l***est branch of the tree. The sw*** is made from two str*** pieces of rope and a wooden seat. Anne likes to play on the sw*** with her friends. While they are play*** they often s*** s***s to each other. Their favourite s***s are ones they learned to s*** at school. Sometimes Anne's friend, Jennifer, sits on the sw***. She is a nervous girl. If Anne pushes the sw*** while Jennifer is sitt*** on it, Jennifer cl***s tightly to the two str*** ropes.

5

ea and **ai**

seat

chain

1. It falls from dark clouds. r**n
2. Most animals have one. t**l
3. We have them while we sleep. dr**ms
4. Another word for robbing. st**ling
5. The opposite of expensive. ch**p
6. A kind of vegetable. b**n
7. Each finger has one. n**l
8. Part of the coast. b**ch
9. Another name for a bucket. p**l
10. T**chers compl**n when children are late.
11. Jean cooked m**t pie, chips and p**s for lunch.
12. There should be no st**ns on cl**n towels.
13. Old r**lways used to have st**m engines.
14. A spr**ned ankle could be very p**nful.
15. Vandals sm**red p**nt over the garden wall.

railway station
painting
train

cleaning
steam engine

6 **ch** and **ce**

tea**ch**er

di**ce**

1. Two robins are sitting on a bran**.
2. Why do cats like to **ase mi**?
3. The boxer was pun**ed on his **in.
4. Whi** men are helping to mend the fen**?
5. Joe will win** if you kick his shin.
6. Henry has no **ance of winning the ra**.
7. The clock **imes twelve times at noon.
8. May I have a sli** of **ocolate cake please?
9. A rubber ball will boun** when it is dropped.
10. I had roast **icken and **ips for lun**.
11. Richard had to **op some logs for the fire.
12. Meat sandwi**es cost more than **eese rolls.
13. There are seven words in this senten**.
14. Grace has a pretty la** handker**ief.
15. **ess is a difficult game for **ildren to play.

16. Richard is a tea**er and his brother, Lance, is an ambulan** driver. The brothers always **oose different things to eat. Ri**ard's first **oice is fish and **ips. Lan** would rather have lamb **ops with fried ri**. Lan** enjoys ri** pudding but Ri**ard prefers sli**d pea**es and cream. Lan** takes ham sandwi**es to work in his lun** box. Ri**ard prefers to have a **eese salad. On coa** outings, Ri**ard takes plenty of **ocolate. Lan** would rather buy an i** cream when the coa** driver stops for a rest.

7

ay and **ow**

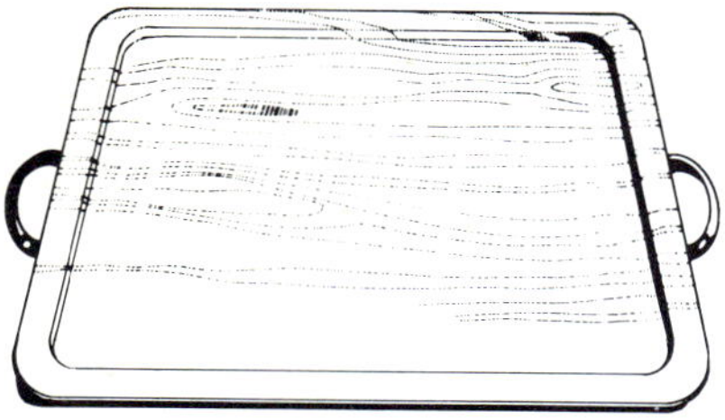

tray

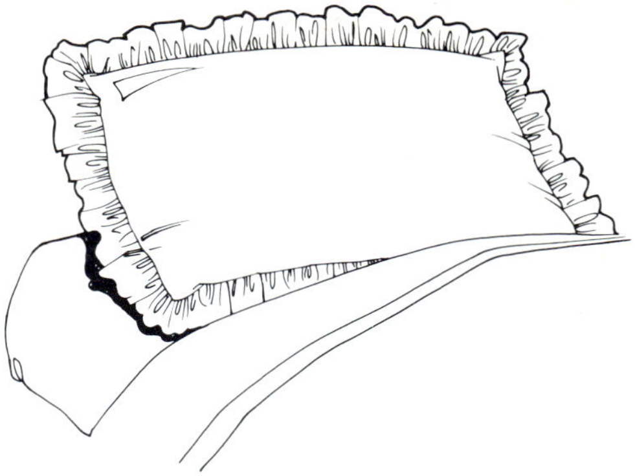

pillow

1. The opposite of never. alw**s
2. It falls during the winter. sn**
3. The lighter part of a day. d**time
4. You may rest your head on one. pill**
5. The opposite of lending. borr**ing
6. A heavy kind of vegetable. marr**
7. Children draw pictures with them. cr**ons
8. A container for soup or porridge. b**l
9. The day before today. yesterd**
10. An arm joint. elb**
11. The side of a road or lane. w**side
12. These men melt in the sun. sn**men
13. Sums of money to be paid. p**ments
14. They can be looked through. wind**s
15. Children play games here. pl**ground

16. Ray is a keen gardener. He gr**s lots of vegetables. His favourite vegetables are marr**s and cucumbers. R** gr**s plants from seeds which he s**s in narr** seed tr**s. He spr**s his plants with a special liquid. The liquid helps to keep insects aw** from the roots and leaves of the plants. R** waters some plants every d** during dry weather. He kn**s his plants m** die if they are not spr**ed regularly with water.

8

ay and **oy**

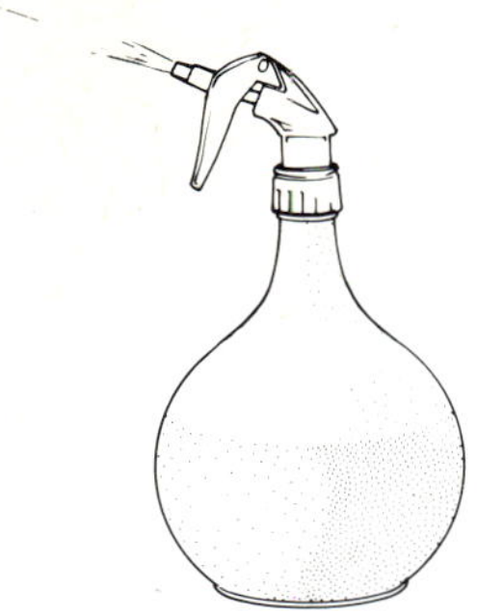

spray

toys

1. J**ce is a girl's name.
2. Royston is a b**'s name.
3. There are seven d**s in a week.
4. A t** is a kind of pl**thing.
5. Never is the opposite of alw**s.
6. Children like to pl** with sand and water.
7. There are many t**s in a toy shop.
8. A netball team has seven pl**ers.
9. The sun only shines during the d**time.
10. Real pearls come from **sters.
11. Large tins have several l**ers of biscuits.
12. The pl**ful kitten plays with a ball of wool.
13. Vandals are people who like to destr** things.
14. One kind of warship is called a destr**er.
15. An empl**er p**s the wages of his workers.

toys
boys
enjoying

holiday
playing
spraying

9

ts and **ce**

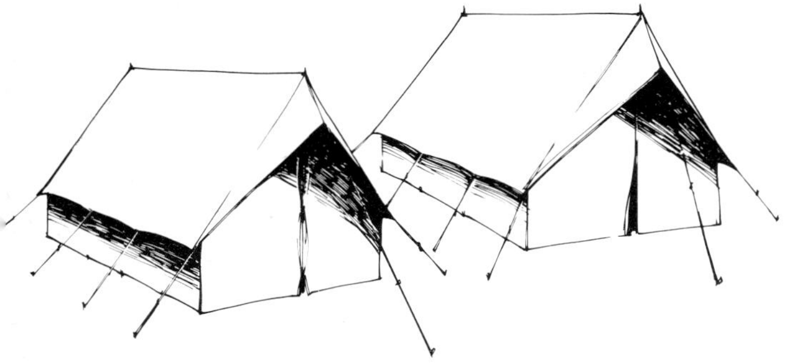

tents

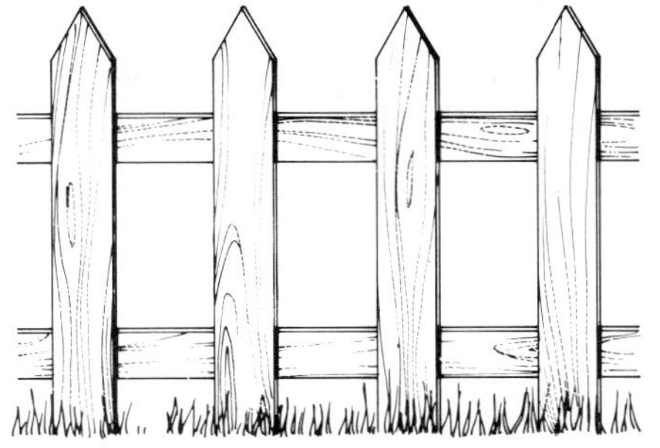

fence

1. Two sheep are standing by the fen**.
2. It has been raining sin** ten o'clock.
3. Most campers sleep in canvas ten**.
4. Can you see any an** on the path?
5. The son of a king or a queen is a prin**.
6. Children like to dan** around a May Pole.
7. Cactus plan** grow in desert lands.
8. Our dog pan** whenever it is very hot.
9. An entran** is the opposite of an exit.
10. There are several elephan** in the zoo.
11. Camels can travel a long distan** without water.
12. A detective examined the conten** of the cabinet.
13. Soldiers advan** slowly towards the enemy camp.
14. The lion hun** for food in the jungle.
15. The judge listened carefully to all the eviden**.

16. Some Boy Scou** are having a camping holiday on a farm. They made sure that there were no an** on the ground before they put up their ten**. There was plenty of space for their ten** near the entran** to the field. Each of the Scou** has the choi** of helping to prepare the food or to wash the po** and pans after the meals. There is a tall fen** between the field and the farm garden. The farmer grows lo** of carro**, potatoes and cabbages. He sells his produ** at the farm shop which is a short distan** from the field where the Scou** are camping.

10

ai and **oa**

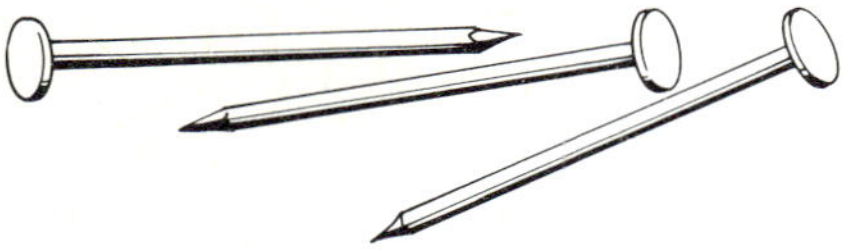

nails

boat

1.	This kind of animal has horns.	g**t
2.	Men and women wear them.	c**ts
3.	A method of transport.	tr**n
4.	We use it when we wash.	s**p
5.	A kind of artist.	p**nter
6.	Anglers use it to attract fish.	b**t

7. We will get wet if it r**ns.
8. Joan has a st**n on her blue c**t.
9. The team scored two g**ls in ten minutes.
10. The w**ter is carrying a st**nless steel tray.
11. Water from the sink pours into a dr**n.
12. Do you know why cork fl**ts on water?
13. The w**tress brought me a p**ched egg on t**st.
14. Rowing b**ts do not have engines or s**ls.
15. Most traffic travels on the m**n r**ds.

coach
road
coats

waitress
waist

11

a-e and **o-e**

spade

rose

1. Please put the c*k*s on the white pl*t*.
2. R*p* is thicker and stronger than string.
3. Jane bought a bunch of green gr*p*s for her mother.
4. Grace keeps two t*m* rabbits as pets.
5. Dave br*k* his wrist when he fell off the horse.
6. The thief st*l* all the jewels from the s*f*.
7. You will be l*t* if you do not hurry to school.
8. A jet aeropl*n* flies faster than a helicopter.
9. Do you like the new glass lamp sh*d* in the lounge?
10. A clown usually paints his n*s* red.
11. Please cl*s* the door when you leave the room.
12. The small saucepan is on the gas st*v*.
13. Why do th*s* orphans have no mother or father?
14. There is a st*n* cross on the war memorial.
15. Dave g*v* the dog a huge b*n* for its dinner.

16. Dave does not like people to play practical j*k*s on him. He has enough trouble without them. Today he br*k* one of his mother's best pl*t*s. Yesterday he g*v* a b*n* to a dog which promply bit his n*s*. Last week he str*k*d a cat which then scratched his f*c*. Once he was digging with a sp*d* and the handle br*k*. Last year, when he cl*s*d a g*t* he found out that it had just been painted. On another occasion he r*d* his bicycle along a l*n*. The bicycle skidded and he fell straight into a thorny r*s* bush.

12

o-e and **u-e**

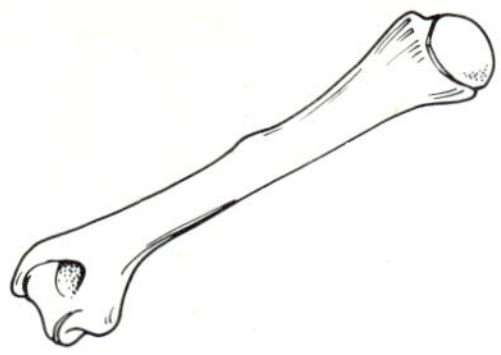

bone

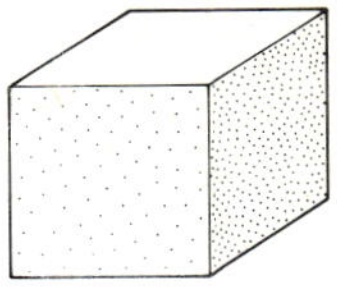

cube

1.	Not polite.	r*d*
2.	The place where you live.	h*m*
3.	An animal which carries loads.	m*l*
4.	The shape of a dice.	c*b*
5.	A funny saying.	j*k*
6.	Part of an electric plug.	f*s*
7.	It has two nostrils.	n*s*
8.	A musical instrument.	fl*t*
9.	You could fall into a big one.	h*l*
10.	This person is a bully.	br*t*
11.	The bottom of a shoe.	s*l*
12.	The opposite of open.	cl*s*d
13.	A dried plum.	pr*n*
14.	This flower grows on a bush.	r*s*
15.	We have these in our hands.	b*n*s

holes rose hose

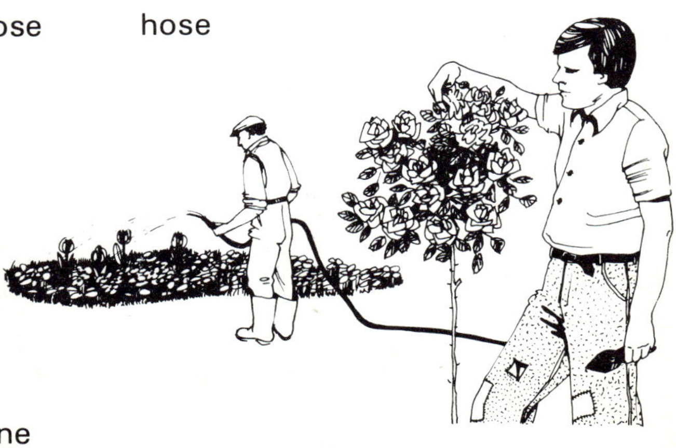

use prune

13

a-e and **u-e**

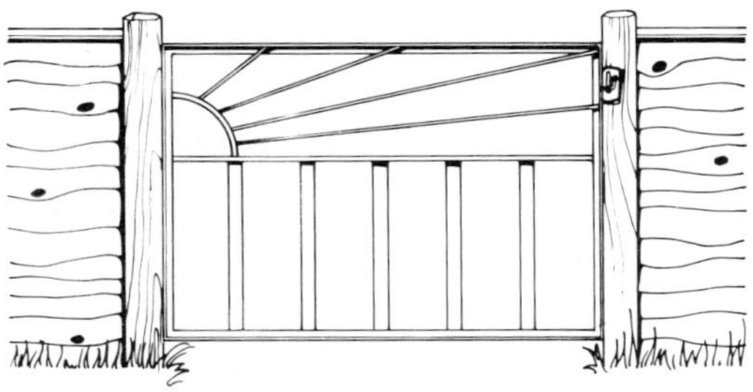

gate

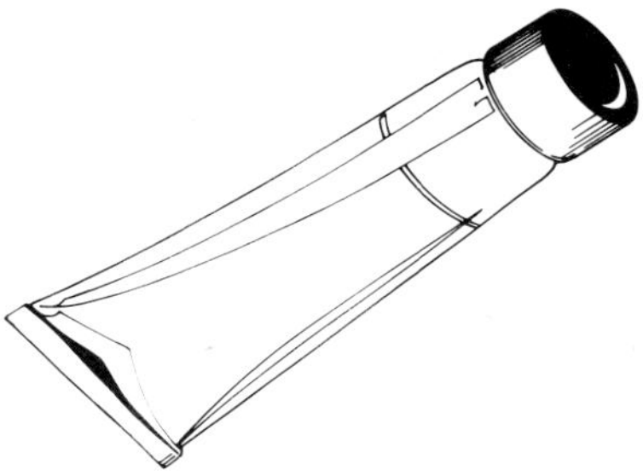

tube

1. The boy's n*m* is Dave.
2. Mother is baking a fruit c*k*.
3. The gas fire has a bright fl*m*.
4. Plenty of fish swim in the l*k*.
5. Why do you hum t*n*s when you are happy?
6. Jane's sisters are Grace and J*n*.
7. Dad uses a sp*d* to dig holes in the garden.
8. Pete broke a p*n* of glass in the window.
9. Kate has a new t*b* of white toothpaste.
10. Each electric plug must have its correct f*s*.
11. Dave is sitting on the wooden farm g*t*.
12. A r*d* boy is one who has bad manners.
13. Luke is playing a t*n* on his fl*t*.
14. J*m*s scratched his f*c* when he fell off his bike.
15. Roof tiles in some countries are made from sl*t*.

16. Dave is a keen gardener. Among his tools D*ve has a sp*d*, a fork and a r*k*. His wife, June, is a good cook. J*n* b*k*s lots of small c*k*s and fruit pies. Her c*k*s are always eaten before they have time to become st*l*. D*v* has two children n*m*d Luke and Kate. Their interests are not the s*m*. K*t* writes t*n*s to play on her fl*t*. Her favourite g*m* is tennis. L*k* breeds t*m* rabbits. He s*v*s all the money when he sells them. L*k* makes model aeropl*n*s and he puts the money towards the cost of his next aeropl*n* kit.

14

i-e and **o-e**

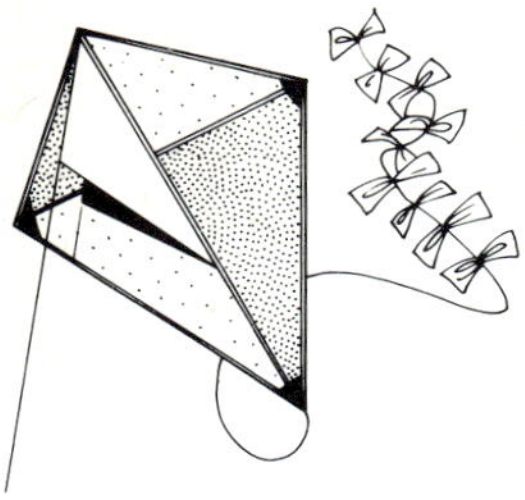

kite

globe

1.	One less than ten.	n*n*
2.	Flags hang from the top of them.	p*l*s
3.	Food is cooked on it.	st*v*
4.	Part of a church.	sp*r*
5.	A ball could roll down one.	sl*p*
6.	Put the p*l* of dishes near the sink.	
7.	Steve threw a st*n* through the window.	
8.	Many children l*k* to drink fizzy lemonade.	
9.	Two workmen are digging a h*l* in the road.	
10.	R*p* grapes are full of sweet juice.	
11.	Mark uses shoe polish to sh*n* his shoes.	
12.	The water on the lake fr*z* quickly last night.	
13.	The angry teacher sp*k* sternly to the children.	
14.	Mike br*k* a finger when he fell off his b*k*.	
15.	The clock bell ch*m*s tw*c* at two o'clock.	

five ribbons   kite   clothes line   bone   pole

15

ee and **oa**

tr**ee**

c**oa**t

1. There are seven days in a w**k.
2. You can hang your c**ts on those hooks.
3. Please fetch a brush and sw**p the path.
4. Would you prefer one or two pieces of t**st?
5. Why are those sh**p standing near the fence?
6. We have two jars of coff** in the pantry.
7. Shall we have r**st b**f for lunch on Sunday?
8. The dentist had to take out the thr** bad t**th.
9. Ch**rful children are usually very happy.
10. People who are humble are never b**stful.
11. Careful children never dash across a r**d.
12. The best toilet s**p contains expensive perfume.
13. Jane's dress is white but Joan's is gr**n.
14. Sailing ships are bigger than rowing b**ts.
15. The c**ch could not go down the narrow str**t.

16. Many farmers in New Zealand br**d sh**p. A few farmers k**p goats. Sh**p provide us with wool and meat. The c**t of a sh**p is called a fl**ce. Wool is made from the fl**ce of sh**p. Woollen c**ts are not cheap and sh**pskin c**ts are very expensive. G**ts are mainly kept for their milk but some farmers use g**ts' milk for making ch**se.

16

ea and **ay**

b**ea**ds

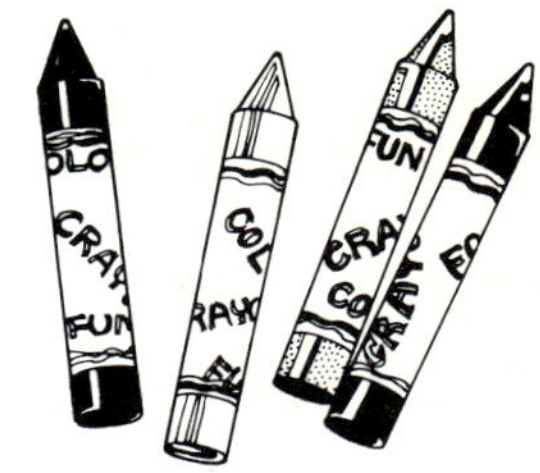

cr**ay**ons

1. We get it from milk.
2. A potter uses it to make pots.
3. It could have a long spout.
4. Two days before tomorrow.
5. It is produced by the sun.
6. Thieves are people who st**l things.
7. Some hens l** large brown eggs.
8. Why do we dr**m while we are asleep?
9. Keep aw** from the edge of the cliff.
10. A man who is m**n is called a miser.
11. Pl**se put the plates on the tr**.
12. Do not light a fire n**r the h** stack.
13. We have to p** for **ch ticket separately.
14. Our t**m is pl**ing aw** from home tod**.
15. Some people st** down on their knees to pr**.

cr**m
cl**
t**pot
yesterd**
d**light

blackboard and easel
teacher
teapot

playing
tray

17

ar and **er**

arch

ladd**er**

1. A c** is small** than a bus.
2. The g**den fork is in the shed.
3. There are sev**al swings in the p**k.
4. Snow is white but t** is black.
5. Bring a packet of butt** from the pantry.
6. Gordon has a stall at the local m**ket.
7. Summ** is hott** than wint**.
8. Were you born in M**ch or Septemb**?
9. Ask the teach** to m**k your work.
10. There are thousands of st**s in the sky.
11. Bert has a splint** in his fing**.
12. A market g**dener is not a cattle f**mer.
13. We cannot afford to buy a new c**pet.
14. The mansion has sev**al m**ble fireplaces.
15. Fath** dropped a spann** und** the bench.

16. L**ge towns sometimes have open-air m**kets. M**kets have stalls selling many diff**ent kinds of goods. The m**ket in Newtown is open ev**y week-day. One of the busiest stalls sells c**pets and floor cov**ings. The next stall stocks cheap shoes and slipp**s. An attractive stall is the one which sells birthday c**ds and sheets of pretty wrapping pap**. Two broth**s have been selling wallpap** with many diff**ent patt**ns for sev**al years. Before wint** arrives, the busiest stall in the m**ket is the one which sells a wide range of sweat**s, jump**s, pullov**s and c**digans at b**gain prices.

18

oa and **ou**

coach

blouse

1. Made from bread.
2. They are seen in the sky.
3. A little animal with a long tail.
4. Clothing worn by girls.
5. It is similar to a frog.
6. A method of cooking beef.
7. The edge of an island.
8. A mansion is a kind of large h**se.
9. Please buy me an extra l**f of bread.
10. A television ann**ncer must have a clear voice.
11. Children sh**t to each other in the playgr**nd.
12. Did you go on the c**ch **ting yesterday?
13. I c**nted eight men working on the fishing b**t.
14. Joan w**nd the rope ar**nd the gate post.
15. The farmer f**nd two g**ts among his sheep.

t**st
cl**ds
m**se
bl**ses
t**d
r**sting
c**st

goat
boat

house
clouds
mountain

19

ar and **or**

car

fork

1. H**d is the opposite of soft.
2. I need a new battery f** my t**ch.
3. F**mers store their hay in b**ns.
4. Mark and Norman are playing football in the p**k.
5. Mother has stitched a patch on my t**n jacket.
6. Can you find a c**k to fit this bottle?
7. Gordon's al**m clock has a loud buzzer.
8. M**ch is the month between February and April.
9. Children who are st**ving feel very hungry.
10. The secretary asked me to sign the f**m.
11. Twelve ships came into the p**t last week.
12. Sp**ks should not come from an electric fire.
13. We cannot aff**d to have a long holiday this year.
14. Martha could not st**t her car engine this m**ning.
15. The teacher has a l**ge ass**tment of crayons.

16. Norman Parkinson is a f**mer. He travels around the countryside on his h**se and c**t. It was very d**k last night. The st**s were hidden by d**k rain clouds. A st**m had left the road very wet and slippery. N**man had turned the c**ner from the road into his farmy**d when he heard the hooting of a car h**n. With the aid of his t**ch, N**man was able to see that a c** had skidded into a ditch. The driver of the c** was f**tunate that Norman had heard the h**n. Because he had broken both **ms, the driver could not have got out of his c** without help.

20

a-e and **i-e**

sc**a**l**e**s

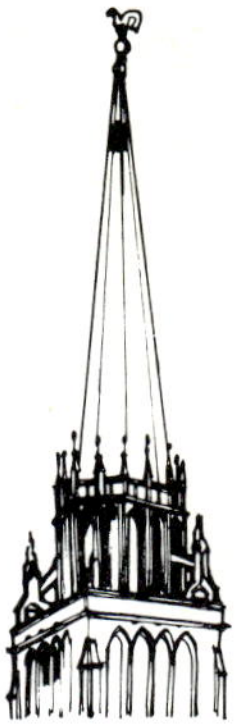

sp**i**r**e**

1.	The opposite of black.	wh*t*
2.	Go into water head first.	d*v*
3.	A very strong wind.	g*l*
4.	They help to keep houses warm.	f*r*s
5.	Men do this with razors.	sh*v*
6.	Strike a match if you want one.	fl*m*
7.	It goes to a point above a church.	sp*r*
8.	Fill something with air.	infl*t*
9.	A kind of food made with batter.	panc*k*
10.	Adders, cobras and vipers.	sn*k*s
11.	Sounds made by ringing bells.	ch*m*s
12.	Goods are weighed on them.	sc*l*s
13.	Fruit often given to sick people.	gr*p*s
14.	A piece of unexpected news.	surpr*s*
15.	Athletes need this to keep fit.	exerc*s*

16. Children love to play m*k*-believe g*m*s. Little girls wear wh*t* dresses and pretend that they are br*d*s. Small boys pretend that they can sh*v* l*k* their fathers. Older children fly k*t*s in the sky and imagine that they are aeropl*n* pilots. Actors and actresses do the s*m* sort of thing when they work on a st*g*. It is part of their work to pretend that they are other people.

21

oo and **ie**

book

ties

1. Insects with wings. fl**s
2. Useful for sweeping a path. br**m
3. These are not true. l**s
4. A small stream. br**k
5. Pigs live in them. st**s
6. A kind of dog. p**dle
7. It covers a building. r**f
8. The baby cr**s because she is hungry.
9. Cr**ks are people who cannot be trusted.
10. Terry tr**d to do the difficult sums.
11. A warm breeze s**n dr**s damp clothes.
12. L**k both ways before you cross a road.
13. David den**d that he had stolen the b**k.
14. People l**k at old things in museums.
15. A carpenter tr**d to repair the w**den desk.

cooker
book
broom

pies
fried

22

oi and **oo**

boiler

boots

1.	The opposite of bad.	g**d
2.	A person who is foolish.	f**l
3.	A kind of water heater.	b**ler
4.	Many children like to read them.	b**ks
5.	Metal pieces of money.	c**ns
6.	You can buy it from a chemist.	**ntment
7.	Elbows, knees and ankles.	j**nts
8.	A few old churches have cr**ked spires.	
9.	It is rude to p**nt with your finger.	
10.	Use a br**m to sweep the s**l off the path.	
11.	A game hunter tries to sh**t wild animals.	
12.	Can you hear the sound of the owl h**ting?	
13.	Keep bottles of p**son away from children.	
14.	The dress shop has a g**d ch**ce of skirts.	
15.	H**ligans try to sp**l other people's pleasure.	

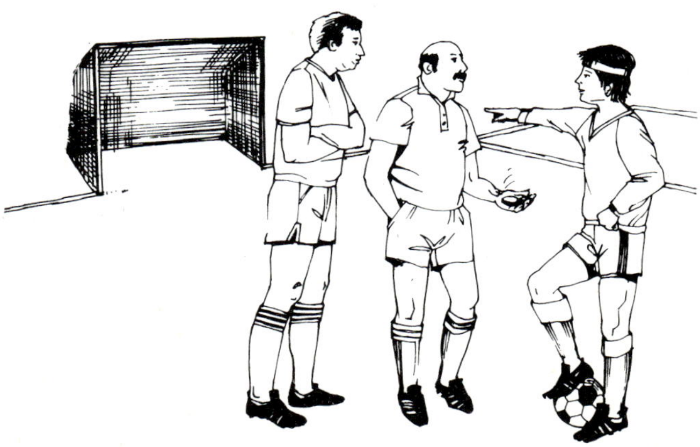

coin
pointing

boots
foot
football

23

ow and **oo**

cr**ow**n

f**oo**tball

1. A br**m has a long w**den handle.
2. Twelve people st**d in a queue for the bus.
3. Circus cl**ns try to be funny men.
4. The c** jumped over the m**n.
5. Children enjoy reading g**d story b**ks.
6. A gang of cr**ks robbed the bank.
7. Why do some f**ls lay br**n eggs?
8. H** many c**ks work in the hotel kitchen?
9. Wendy put the fl**ers in the dining-r**m.
10. David is sc**ling because he is upset.
11. Susan is smiling because she is in a g**d m**d.
12. The police are l**king d**n into the cellar.
13. The b**ts are t** small for Eric to wear.
14. We expect g**d c**ks to prepare appetising meals.
15. Norman t**k a dive into the swimming p**l.

16. Many t**ns have one or more swimming p**ls. Open-air p**ls do not have a r**f and can only be used in fine weather. The covered p**ls can be used all the year round. Some p**ls have sh**ers which the swimmers can use after they have finished their time in the p**l. Swimmers stand under the sh**ers and wash themselves with the c**l water.

24

ar and **ow**

dart

tower

1.	The opposite of up.	d**n
2.	The outside part of a tree.	b**k
3.	It helps to get things dry.	t**el
4.	A place where goods are sold.	m**ket
5.	The colour of soil.	br**n
6.	Two people who work together.	p**tners
7.	Beautiful plants.	fl**ers

8. The old f**mer uses a horse and c**t.
9. H** many st**s are in the sky?
10. Most cl**ns wear funny costumes and hats.
11. A packet of soap p**der is under the sink.
12. Can you hear the al**m bell ringing?
13. The tall t**er has a spiral staircase.
14. Cats pr**l around g**dens in the d**k.
15. C**penters know h** to sh**pen their tools.

cart
market
bargains

crowd
flowers

25

ai and **ow**

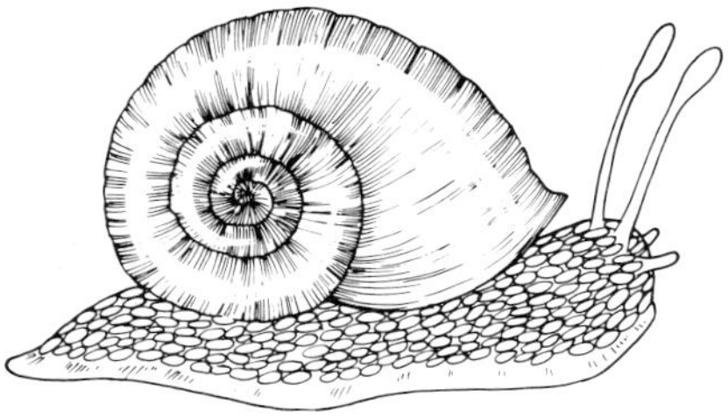

snail

clown

1. A bee sting can be very p**nful.
2. Bath t**els are bigger than tea t**els.
3. Jack fell d**n and broke his cr**n.
4. June is wearing a pl**n br**n costume.
5. Most cl**ns work in travelling circuses.
6. I feel f**nt because the sun is so hot.
7. Charles has a gold cr**n and a silver ch**n.
8. The players had a hot sh**er after the game.
9. A s**ling boat is ch**ned to the jetty.
10. Compl**n to the w**ter if your meal is cold.
11. Mark has a br**n st**n on his trousers.
12. Daisy ch**ns are made from d**sy fl**ers.
13. Cr**ds of people are w**ting for the tr**ns.
14. The br**n r**ncoat has leather buttons.
15. Some p**nts are a mixture of p**der and water.

16. Mrs. Brown lives in an old house near the centre of a large t**n. Her son bought her an oil p**nting for her birthday. It was mounted in a large br**n wooden frame. The p**nting was of a farming scene. There were some f**ls pecking at gr**ns of seed. Severals c**s were sitting on the ground. The farmer wore a badly st**ned jacket and the milk-maid wore a br**n overall. She was carrying a p**l of milk from the c**shed.

26

Long vowels

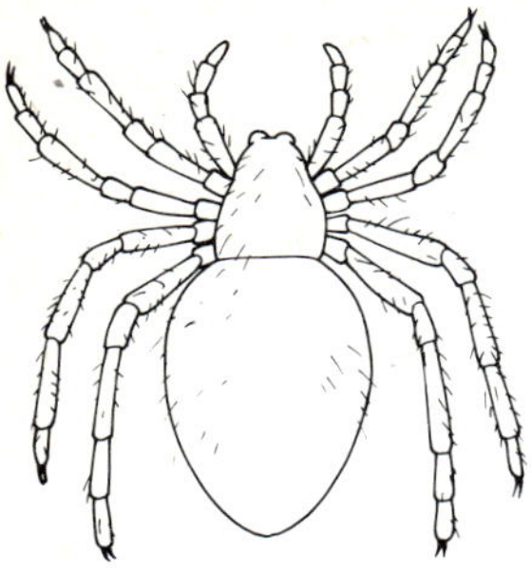

sp**i**der

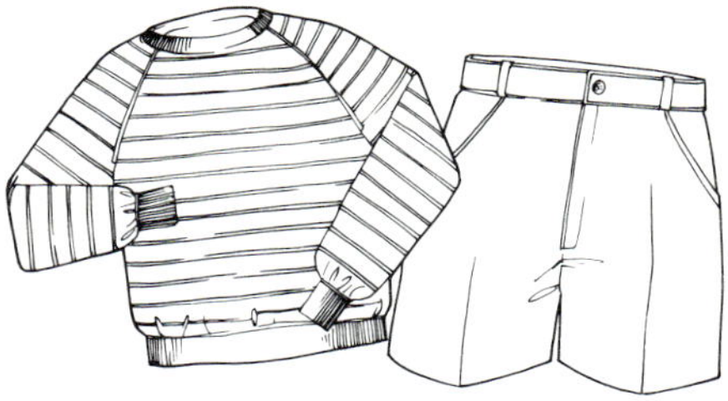

cl**o**thes

t**a**ble

1.	A young male horse.	c*lt
2.	They usually have four legs.	t*bles
3.	A kind of small horse.	p*ny
4.	Sounds made with musical instruments.	m*sic
5.	Not long ago.	r*cent

6. Do you like the t*ste of mustard?
7. Closed is the opposite of *pen.
8. Shall we go for a str*ll through the park?
9. The knives are on the d*ning-room t*ble.
10. Please help me to f*nd the g*ld wedding ring.
11. Do not pour gr*vy *ver the b*ked pot*toes.
12. Shall I fry two sl*ces of sm*ked b*con?
13. M*st airline p*lots wear blue *niforms.
14. Coal and gas are different k*nds of f*el.
15. The hor*zon is not clear on a h*zy day.

lady soldier rifle
tunic baby holding

27

aw and **ew**

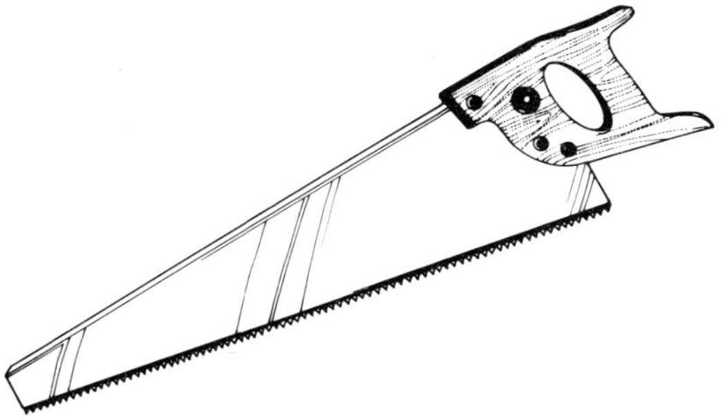

saw

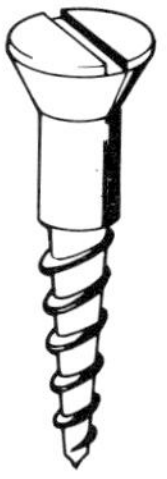

screw

1. The dog is licking its p**.
2. Used clothes are not n**.
3. People are expected to obey the l**.
4. F** is the opposite of many.
5. A flock of birds fl** over the trees.
6. We use our j**s whenever we ch** food.
7. Mother cried when she heard the bad n**s.
8. Father keeps all his s**s in the garage.
9. Richard always seems to be ch**ing toffees.
10. D**n is the opposite of dusk.
11. The old parrot has long sharp cl**s.
12. Mandy is wearing a n** str** hat.
13. The baby is cr**ling across the l**n.
14. Paul thr** a f** snowballs at Timothy.
15. The sheriff kn** where the outl** was hiding.

16. Norman is a skilled carpenter. He makes n** furniture for a f** large furniture shops. He has several s**s with very sharp teeth and some good scr**drivers. Norman needs the scr**drivers and metal scr**s to join large pieces of wood together. He uses glue instead of scr**s when he makes dr**ers for small cabinets. Norman likes to make small j**el boxes which he gives to his friends as presents.

28 **ee** and **ou**

sh**ee**p

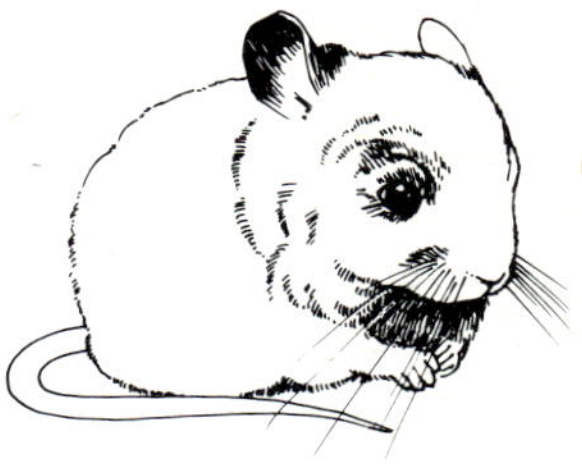

m**ou**se

1.	It has roots and branches.	tr**
2.	An article of girls clothing.	bl**se
3.	The colour of fresh grass.	gr**n
4.	Rubber balls do this.	b**nce
5.	The opposite of shallowest.	d**pest
6.	Often done by people with colds.	sn**zing
7.	Part of a teapot or a kettle.	sp**t
8.	This animal does not like cats.	m**se
9.	There are two on most beds.	sh**ts
10.	A game usually played by girls.	r**nders
11.	The number which follows fifteen.	sixt**n
12.	Solid food made from milk.	ch**se
13.	The line marked around an area.	b**ndary
14.	Sugar gives this to food.	sw**tness
15.	An ornament which uses water.	f**ntain

16. Wealthy sh**p farmers in Australia own th**sands of sh**p. In m**ntainous areas the sh**p spend all their lives on the m**ntains. Sh**p feed better in the valleys where the grass is gr**ner.

Farmers use sh**p-dogs to help them r**nd up the sheep. A good sh**p-dog will save its master c**ntless h**rs of work every year. Dogs can travel over rough gr**nd very easily and they can soon r**nd up any stray sheep.

29 ow and aw

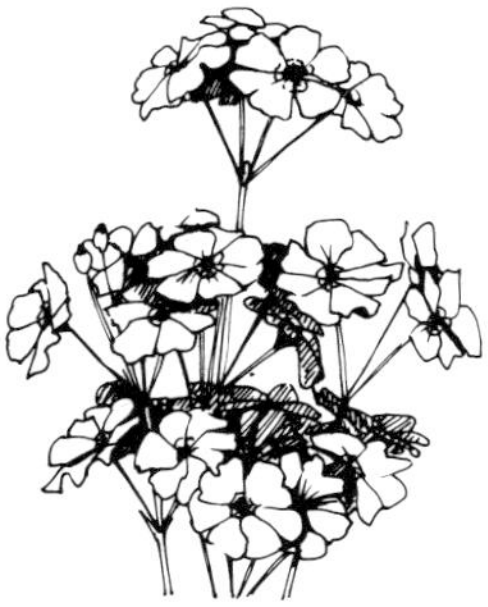

flowers

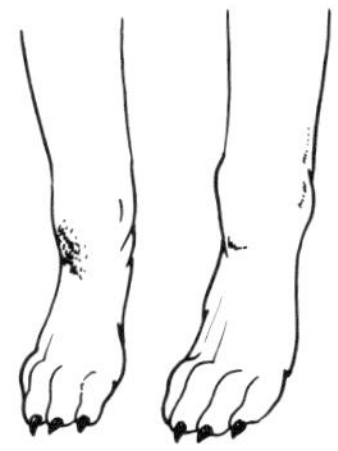

paws

1. Up is the opposite of d**n.
2. My l**n mower has sharp blades.
3. Sports cars have p**erful engines.
4. The bus is cr**ded with children.
5. The baby is cr**ling across the room.
6. Do you like my br**n woollen jumper?
7. Some dogs eat r** meat off a bone.
8. Why do churches have tall spires or t**ers?
9. The old lady wears a white lace sh**l.
10. Criminals are people who do not obey the l**.
11. If you cannot swim you could dr**n in deep water.
12. Do you think that bagpipes make an **ful noise?
13. Crocodiles have many sharp teeth in their j**s.
14. I s** your sister in the t**n centre yesterday.
15. A jackd** is perched on the window ledge.

clown

owl

drawer

shawl

jaws

30

eigh and **ough**

Jane is w**eigh**ing herself. John th**ough**t he was safe.

1. Seven and one. ****t
2. The sound made by a horse. n****
3. Goods carried on ships or trains. fr****t
4. It might be pulled by a reindeer. sl****
5. They come into your mind. th****ts
6. The number which stands for nothing. n****t
7. We ****t to catch the train if we hurry.
8. The lioness f****t to protect her cubs.
9. Claire b****t some stockings at the market.
10. Dawn hopes to become engaged when she is ****teen.
11. Kind people are always very th****tful.
12. Edna has br****t some sandwiches for our lunch.
13. Our grandfather will be ****ty-five next week.
14. Scientists must w**** chemicals accurately.
15. Faulty w****ing machines show incorrect w****ts.

sleigh freight eight noughts thoughtful

31

dge and **tch**

bri**dge**

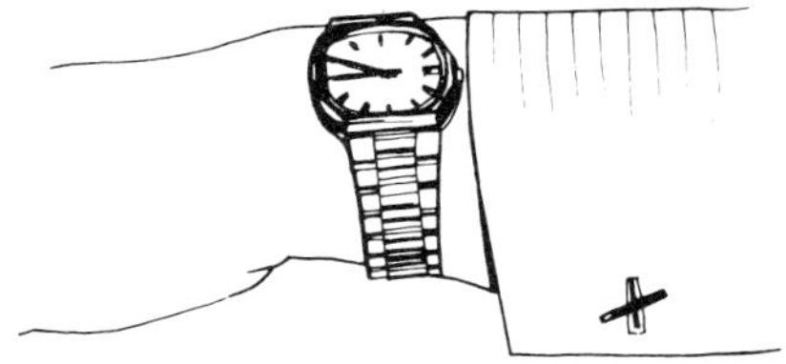

wa**tch**

1. The poor boy has a pa*** on his trousers.
2. Children should not play with ma***es.
3. Sweet shops sell packets of caramel fu***.
4. Joe's rabbit hu*** is made of wood and wire.
5. Slu*** is another name for thick mud.
6. Keep away from the e*** of the quarry.
7. Ruth has a smu*** of lipstick on her cheek.
8. Madge carries her books to school in a sa***el.
9. Sle***hammers are used for breaking rocks.
10. A he***hog's body is covered with prickles.
11. The wicked wi*** wore a pointed black hat.
12. A foot-bri*** goes across the narrow gorge.
13. Reindeers can pull sle***s over snow.
14. A crippled girl may need to use cru***es.
15. The thief tried to sna*** a lady's purse.

16. Madge works in a bu***er's shop on the e*** of a small village. One day a thief sna***ed a gold wa*** from her handbag. One of her customers chased the thief and tried to ca*** him. The thief threw the wa*** into a di*** and ran towards a bri***. The customer managed to ca*** the thief before he crossed the bri***. Another man fe***ed a policeman who took the thief to the police station. The customer found the wa*** which had landed in a di***. Ma*** gave him a reward when he returned the wa*** to her.

32

air and **ear**

ch**air**

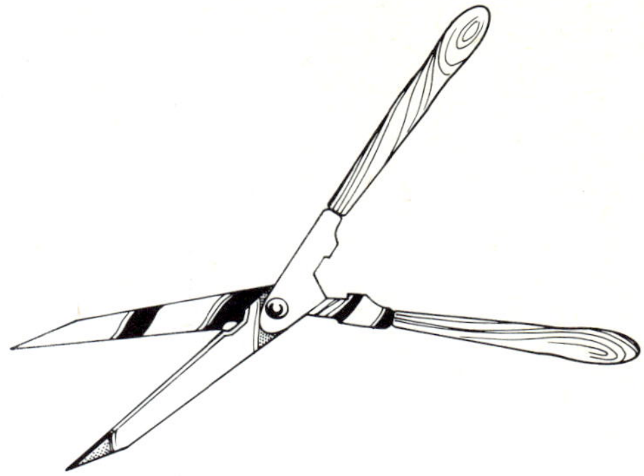

sh**ear**s

1. We have two of these. ***s
2. A piece of furniture. ch***
3. It is breathed into lungs. ***
4. An old-fashioned weapon. sp***
5. We make them when we cry. t***s
6. You can see the sun on a cl*** day.
7. We h*** sounds with our ***s.
8. Watch-makers can rep*** broken watches.
9. Many passengers arrive at busy ***ports.
10. Most modern bicycles have g***s to change.
11. Cut the hedge with a p*** of sh***s.
12. The d***est seats are n*** to the stage.
13. My h***dresser is always busy on Saturdays.
14. Conjurers make rabbits disapp*** from their hats.
15. A spiral st***case is not straight.

hair chair pair shears near

33

ie and **ea**

ties

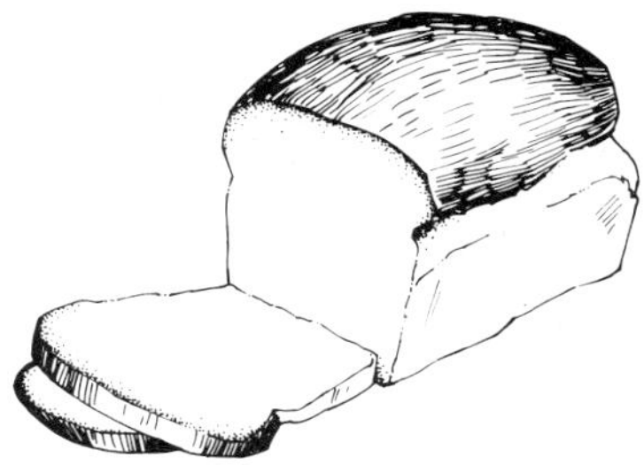

bread

1. The baby cr**s whenever she is upset.
2. Farmers keep their pigs in pig st**s.
3. Maud slipped and hurt her h**d when she fell.
4. Do you prefer brown or white br**d?
5. Washing dr**s quickly on a fine day.
6. Sp**s try to steal other people's secrets.
7. Margaret tr**d to bake a cake for her mother.
8. The best shoes are made from good l**ther.
9. An aeroplane usually fl**s above the clouds.
10. Dr**d milk does not taste like fresh milk.
11. Angela's favourite meal is fr**d chicken and chips.
12. A w**lthy person is one who is very rich.
13. Scotsmen often eat porridge for their br**kfast.
14. Nervous children dr**d visits to the dentist.
15. It is true that d**d men tell no l**s.

16. Martha is a cook. She cooks br**kfast for people who work at a l**ther factory. She fr**s hundreds of eggs every week. The men like to have slices of fr**d br**d with their eggs. Fr**d bacon and sausages are very popular too.
The factory makes l**ther handbags and footw**r. The soft l**ther slippers are very acceptable as birthday presents. Special d**s are used to give the l**ther various colours. Thin strips of soft l**ther are fastened together to make attractive belts. Girls use the belts when they w**r thick woollen sw**ters.

34

are and **ore**

h**are**

apple c**ore**

1. This animal is like a rabbit. h***
2. A kind of shop. st***
3. They burn in the sky. fl***s
4. The centre of an apple. c***
5. Something kept in reserve. sp***
6. Julie w*** her white coat yesterday.
7. Rich men can afford to buy r*** objects.
8. Tommy t*** his sleeve on the wire fence.
9. Pay the exact f*** when you enter the bus.
10. Children who are b***d become restless.
11. The farmer warned us to bew*** of the bull.
12. Adventurers may expl*** caves or jungles.
13. C***ful workers do not make many mistakes.
14. W***houses are buildings where goods are st***d.
15. Farmers depend on accurate weather f***casts.

wore
before
store

spare wheel
carefully

35

ear and **our**

children l**ear**ning

f**our**

1. Something which you own. — y***s
2. The opposite of late. — ***ly
3. The number between three and five. — f***
4. A person who makes a tour. — t***ist
5. The world on which we live. — ***th
6. Children do this at school. — l***n
7. Criminals meet judges here. — c***t
8. A journey through several countries. — t***
9. It has twelve months. — y***
10. Once a year. — y***ly
11. A heavy fall of rain. — downp***
12. Money received for work done. — ***nings
13. A contest between competitors. — t***nament
14. It describes pots made from earth. — ***then
15. Horses between one and two years old. — y***lings

16. There are f*** children in the Smith family. Wendy is a student. She works as a t***ist guide during her summer holidays. She is l***ning about hairdressing at a college. Peter is a lawyer. Much of his time is spent in c***ts. David is a professional tennis player. He ***ns his living by competing in tennis t***naments. Mark is f***teen years old. He gets up ***ly every morning to deliver newspapers before he goes to school.

36

ie and **ea**

sh**ie**ld

f**ea**ther

1.	The opposite of alive.	d**d
2.	These used to protect soldiers.	sh**lds
3.	Part of your body.	h**d
4.	A very heavy metal.	l**d
5.	This person is a leader.	ch**f

6. Br**f intervals last a short time.
7. Brown br**d costs more than white br**d.
8. The farmer is harvesting a f**ld of wheat.
9. H**lthy people do not need to take medicines.
10. A pr**st is a man who helps people to worship.
11. Aspirins may give rel**f from h**daches.
12. The w**ther is warmer during the summer months.
13. Many children eat cornflakes for br**kfast.
14. Very young children bel**ve in fairy stories.
15. Susan is gr**ving because her pony is d**d.

head
sweater

thief
shield
handkerchief

37

ow and **oy**

window

boy

1. The sl**est runner finished the race last.
2. J**ce and R**ston are sister and brother.
3. Only foolish people try to ann** bulls.
4. Wind** cleaners often stand on ladders.
5. The criminal tried to destr** the evidence.
6. A painter uses a bl**lamp to burn off paint.
7. A good empl**er treats his workers fairly.
8. **sters live at the bottom of the sea.
9. L**al people will not betray their country.
10. The sailors went on a v**age around the world.
11. My father enj**s gr**ing huge marr**s.
12. Most b**s enj** thr**ing sn**balls.
13. The hotel uses yell** sheets and pill**-cases.
14. A mixture of two metals is called an all**.
15. Royston keeps his wheel-barr** under the wind**.

16. Some countries have plenty of sn** every winter. Other countries never have any sn**. Sn** is like soft frozen rain. It falls from the clouds in the form of sn**flakes. Each sn**flake has a different pattern. Most b**s love to play with sn**. Some b**s enj** thr**ing sn**balls at each other. Naughty b**s like to ann** girls by thr**ing sn**balls at them. Girls have more enj**ment in using the sn** to make giant sn**men.

38

au and **oe**

s**au**cepan

h**oe**

1.	Parts of feet.	t**s
2.	A tool for weeding gardens.	h**
3.	Not working properly.	f**lty
4.	The place where sheets are washed.	l**ndry
5.	People who are very brave.	her**s
6.	Greengrocers sell them.	tomat**s
7.	It gives extra flavour to food.	s**ce
8.	A cooking utensil.	s**cepan
9.	Artists paint them around saints' heads.	hal**s

10. Ghosts are supposed to live in h**nted houses.
11. Large potat**s are best for making fried chips.
12. The angry lion tried to m**l the lion-tamer.
13. Witches' c**ldrons are large cooking pots.
14. Your voice ech**s when you shout down a well.
15. Rolls of bandage are made from cotton g**ze.

saucepans
bottles of sauce

tomatoes
potatoes

39

ou and **ew**

h**ou**se

n**ew**spaper

1. The children had a hot st** for their dinner.
2. David c**nted over a hundred crayons in the box.
3. Very f** people are able to live in palaces.
4. Why do black cl**ds contain a lot of rain?
5. Children should not ch** gum in the classroom.
6. The boy who f**nd the watch was given a reward.
7. Some people buy a n**spaper every morning.
8. The sailors working on a ship are called the cr**.
9. N** shirts should be washed before they are worn.
10. Children queue to drink water from the f**ntain.
11. The referee bl** his whistle to stop the game.
12. Andrew thr** a small coin on the gr**nd.
13. The angry women sh**ted at the rude boys.
14. Do not lean against the glass c**nter.
15. M**nt Everest is the world's highest m**ntain.

16. People sell n**spapers on the streets of big cities. They sh**t **t the name of the n**spaper as l**dly as they can. Today's n**spaper gives n**s ab**t a robbery at a j**eller's shop. When the j**ellery shop manager arrived for work this morning he f**nd that the safe had been forced open. Th**sands of valuable old postage stamps and hundreds of j**els had been taken. It took several h**rs to find **t exactly what had been stolen. A police detective f**nd some fingerprints on the safe and a f** footprints on the gr**nd below a broken window. The detective said that he thought he kn** the name of the thief.

40

qu and **ph**

queen

ele**ph**ant

1.	A very large animal.	ele**ant
2.	The opposite of slow.	**ick
3.	Children who have no parents.	or**ans
4.	The noise made by a duck.	**ack
5.	This bird has pretty feathers.	**easant
6.	A lady who reigns over a country.	**een
7.	Water, milk, tea and lemonade.	li**ids
8.	He is not a real person.	**antom
9.	Archers carry their arrows in these.	**ivers
10.	Animals with bushy tails.	s**irrels
11.	Pictures taken with cameras.	**otographs
12.	These hinges need to be oiled.	s**eaking
13.	They are sewn on dresses.	se**ins
14.	It could be a cup or a shield.	tro**y
15.	Frightened pigs do this.	s**eal

16. The **een of a small country lived in a grand palace. She often held ban**ets for important people. Lady guests sometimes wore beautiful dresses covered with se**ins. One day the **een decided to do something for the poor people for a change. She asked her secretary to tele**one a local or**anage and invite all the or**ans to a ban**et of their own. The or**ans were thrilled when they heard of the **een's re**est. They kept the invitation as a secret when their in**isitive school friends en**ired why they were so excited. They refused to answer any **estions until after the great day. Then they told their friends all about the **een's kindness to them.

41

ar and **ir**

ta**r**get

bi**r**d

1. Coal miners are d**ty after a day's work.
2. M**k and B**bara belong to the same family.
3. An ostrich is a b**d which cannot fly.
4. Film st**s are well-known people.
5. St** the porridge with the wooden spoon.
6. Margaret is wearing a blue cotton sk**t.
7. A st**ling has her nest in that roof.
8. Some f**mers breed l**ge herds of cattle.
9. The f**st person past the post wins the race.
10. The th**sty children wanted a drink of water.
11. Paul's new sh**t has a stiff collar.
12. The old railway bridge has three **ches.
13. C**go ships carry freight in their holds.
14. The **cher shot an arrow at the t**get.
15. The next train will dep**t at three o'clock.

16. Mark has a l**ge aviary where he breeds beautiful b**ds. He has th**ty budgerig**s and a few mina b**ds. The mina b**ds belong to the st**ling family. M**k never lets his aviary become d**ty. His f**st job each morning is to clear the d**t from the bottom of the aviary. Then he changes the b**ds' drinking water. The b**ds drink clean water from special j**s fixed to the sides of the aviary. Th**dly, he fills the food containers with new b**d seed. The b**ds ch**p excitedly whenever M**k visits them.

42

tion and **ture**

$$\frac{2}{3} \quad \frac{8}{9} \quad \frac{6}{8} \quad \frac{3}{4}$$

frac**tions**

pic**ture**

1. Another name for a holiday. — vaca****
2. They are hung on walls. — pic****s
3. Flat tyres have them. — punc****s
4. A story which is not real. — fic****
5. The place where roads meet. — junc****
6. A break in a bone. — frac****
7. Thirds, quarters and tenths. — frac****s
8. A set of false teeth. — den****s
9. It is measured with a thermometer. — tempera****
10. Some inven****s help to save lives.
11. The best quality furni**** is made from real wood.
12. There is plenty of ac**** during a boxing match.
13. Drive with cau**** if the road is slippery.
14. There is an old marble sculp**** in the museum.
15. Mother gave Richard a big por**** of meat pie.

junction
reflection

furniture
picture
sculpture

43

oi and **ur**

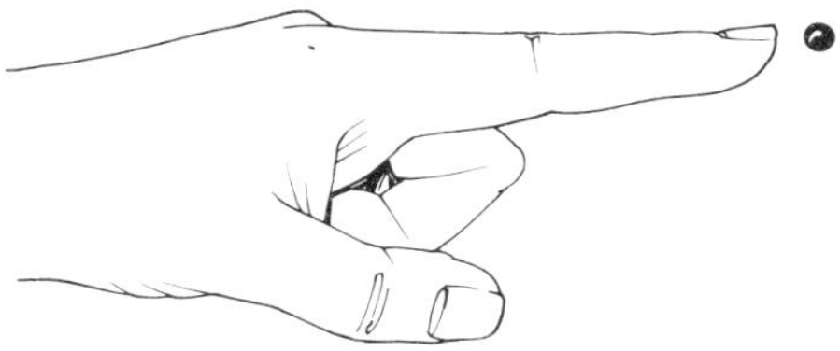

p**oi**nt

ch**ur**ch

1. Steam engines make a hissing n**se.
2. Why do pigs have c**ly tails?
3. You should not p**nt with your finger.
4. People who drop litter sp**l the countryside.
5. Farmers used to make butter in wooden ch**ns.
6. Elizabeth is wearing a genuine f** coat.
7. Angela works in a children's n**sery.
8. The b**ning fat made an awful smell.
9. Keep bottles of p**son in a locked cupboard.
10. Helen took the dirty c**tains to the laundry.
11. Most factories are closed on Sat**days.
12. A n**se put some **ntment on the scratch.
13. The leather p**se was full of gold c**ns.
14. Which shop gives the best ch**ce of c**tains?
15. Christians go to ch**ch on Sundays.

16. Margaret is a n**se. B**ling water helps to keep her uniform a bright white. She always b**ls her clothes in a b**ler before she washes them.
One day her young daughter put her hand on the b**ler. She b**ned her fingers because the b**ler was full of b**ling water. She screamed at the top of her v**ce because her fingers were h**ting so much. When Margaret saw what had happened she put some soothing **ntment on the fingers. They did not h**t so much then.

44

ue and **ou**

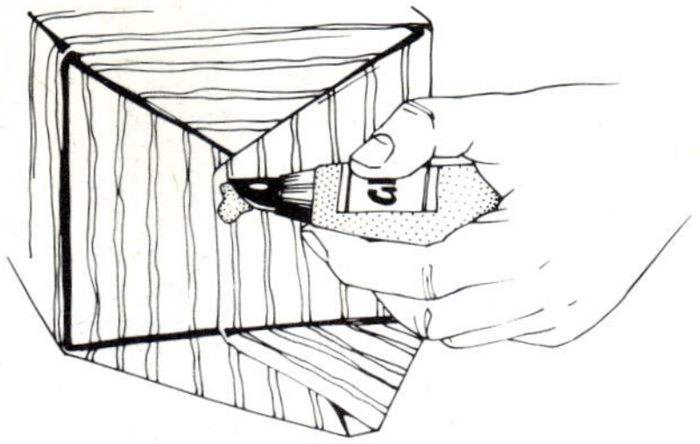

gl**ue**

d**ou**ble '2'

1. The colour of the sea and sky. bl**
2. It sticks things together. gl**
3. We use our fingers to do this. t**ch
4. The opposite of old. y**ng
5. The son of an uncle. c**sin
6. They help to solve mysteries. cl**s
7. Husbands and wives. c**ples
8. The land in which you live. c**ntry
9. Shipwrecked people hope for this. resc**
10. Do not stop. contin**
11. It takes away smoke from a fire. fl**
12. Naughty children often cause this. tr**ble
13. Wise people choose this kind of meal. n**rishing
14. Snooker players use these. c**s
15. Something which ought to be paid. d**

16. Wendy and Claire are c**sins who live in the c**ntry. They helped an old c**ple who lived in a quaint cottage to paint their garden gate. They chose a bl** paint. A y**ng boy called at the cottage soon after the painting was finished. When his coat t**ched the gate the paint stuck like gl** to his sleeve.
The y**ng boy was upset because he thought he would be in tr**ble when he got home. The c**ple telephoned his mother to explain what had happened. Because she knew the story was tr**, his mother was not cross with the y**ng boy when he gave her his account of the accident.

45

ture and **sion**

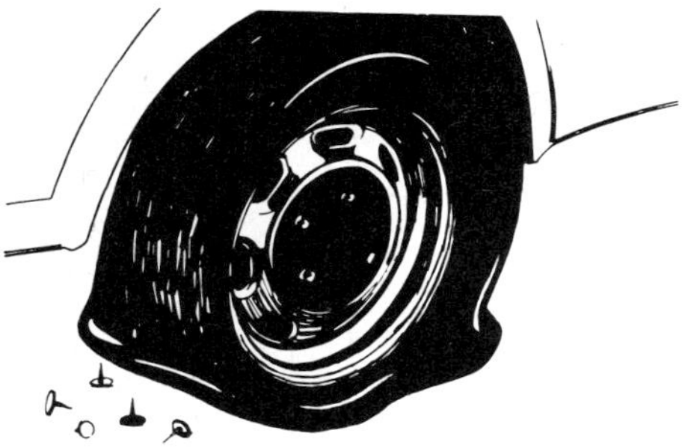

punc**ture**

televi**sion**

1. Arrival is the opposite of depar****.
2. Many homes have a colour televi**** set.
3. Vul****s are birds which feed on dead flesh.
4. Birthday parties are usually happy occa****s.
5. Many pic****s are displayed at Art Galleries.
6. Game hunters try to cap**** wild animals.
7. Children ask for permis**** to leave the room.
8. Philip frac****d his arm when he fell.
9. Children enjoy games in adven**** playgrounds.
10. Some wealthy people live in country man****s.
11. Many firms give pen****s to their retired workers.
12. There was a colli**** at the junction yesterday.
13. An explo**** happened when the plane crashed.
14. Some modern sculp****s are made of concrete.
15. Show your admis**** ticket at the entrance.

16. There was a colli**** between two vans at a busy road junction. A televi**** van was in colli**** with a furni**** van. The televi**** van had collided with the furniture van after it had a punc**** in one of its tyres. The furni**** van was badly damaged and some of its furni**** was smashed to pieces. The police put up diver**** signs until the road was cleared. The televi**** van driver had frac****d one of his legs. The other driver's den**** had fallen on the ground. He had a peculiar expres**** on his face when he saw one of the policemen tread on his den**** and frac**** it. And the expres**** was not a happy one!

46

c (s) and g (j)

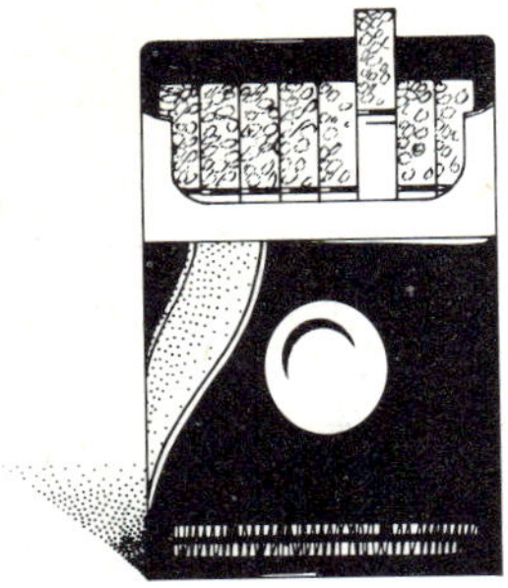

cigarettes

giraffe

1.	Children write with them.	pen*ils
2.	This animal has a long neck.	*iraffe
3.	The daughter of a king and queen.	prin*ess
4.	Disinfectant kills them.	*erms
5.	Buildings where films are shown.	*inemas
6.	One hundred years.	*entury
7.	People who travel a lot.	*ipsies
8.	This is prescribed by doctors.	medi*ine
9.	London is the lar*est *ity in England.	
10.	Ladies expect *entlemen to be polite.	
11.	Smoking *igarettes is a foolish habit.	
12.	Squares, triangles and *ircles are shapes.	
13.	Blondes do not have *inger hair.	
14.	Persons who behave cruelly are mer*iless.	
15.	*enerals are leading army offi*ers.	

circle

dancing

gipsy

giraffe